I0439249

Survival Family Basics

The Prepper's Guide to Survival Food Storage

Macenzie Guiver

Macenzie Guiver

Just to say Thank You for Purchasing this Book I want to give you a gift 100% absolutely FREE

A Copy of My Upcoming Special Report "*The Prepper's Supplies Guide for When Disaster Strikes*"

Go to www.SurvivalFamilyBasics.com to Sign Up to Receive Your FREE Gift

Table of Contents

Introduction

I want to thank you and congratulate you for purchasing the, *Survival Family Basics – The Prepper's Guide to Survival Food Storage.* This book contains proven steps and strategies on how to build emergency food storage for dealing with catastrophes.

The world we live in today is increasingly becoming volatile with each passing day. Terrorism, economic upsets and large scale catastrophes' are situations of real world that have significantly affected our ways of life.

If such a situation occurs, a number of households would run out of food supplies very quickly especially if utility supplies were also affected. Whilst a number of emergencies extend for only a few days, planning for a minimum of fourteen day stay at home possibly without water and electricity ensures that you are prepared for a wide range of circumstances.

It goes without saying that you will probably have no electricity, refrigeration, or gas, so both traditional cooling and cooking facilities would not be available to you. For short term aid, it is important that you have a supply of non-perishable, high energy foods in your disaster pantry.

The concept of being prepared for an emergency situation is not a new one. Since the beginning of human civilization, we have been accustomed to living in a survival mode, actively seeking food, clothing and shelter to keep ourselves safe and protected from the outside environment.

By actively preparing for an emergency crisis in which the basic necessities of life are scarce, you would know exactly what action needs to be taken during a particular situation. How comforting is that?

Having an understanding of this information and being able to utilize it during catastrophic situations could actually mean the difference between life and death. From common mistakes to avoid to comprehensive list of foods that you should store for emergencies, the book will help you learn the preparedness lifestyle by approaching emergency planning and preparedness in a systematic step by step manner.

Thanks again for buying this book. I hope you enjoy it!

Macenzie Guiver

Preparing For Disasters – an Introduction

"Good Planning leads to a good response, and the more planning you have done, the more steadfast you will be in situations like these"

The world we live in today is increasingly unpredictable. The natural and man-made disasters that we continually read and hear about every day through newspaper services remind us that we need to be better prepared for dealing with emergency situations.

Emergencies can occur at any time of the year. From flooding to wind storms to earthquakes to fire outbreaks, even losing your income due to some major accident can be treated as an emergency. We usually do not prepare until the emergency has happened. Food, clothing and shelter are the primary needs that come first when we are confronted with an emergency situation.

Whether the emergency situation lasts for a short period of time or for extended periods, knowing that you are prepared to face it will not only make you self-sufficient but will also bring you peace of mind.

If you ask the manager of a grocery store about how long the supplies would last in case of an emergency crisis, the answer would be three to four days. It is because grocery stores do not usually keep an ample stock of food supplies. When catastrophe strikes, people facing the threat of food and water shortage tend to panic and storm the grocery stores in order to buy supplies they can get.

Should natural disaster, famine or a terrorist attack prevent your access to grocery stores, you should be able to handle these emergencies well. Have you ever imagined what you would do if you had to live on the food available in your pantry for an extended period of time.

What would you do if a disaster strikes today? You could be confined to your home; you could even be confined to your home without basic necessities such as food, water, gas and electricity. Have you ever imagined would you be able to survive if basic utilities were cut off? These are the basic questions that we often leave overlooked. Whilst emergency teams and relief workers respond quickly in case situations like these happen, everyone cannot be helped right away.

Planning ahead of time for situations during which you many need an emergency food supply is a good idea. Understanding how much and which foods to store depends upon various factors including the total number of family members in your household, your preferences, space available for storage, special health conditions and the distance of your home from the market. Keeping an emergency food pantry that is stocked with foods to help you get by until the catastrophic event has passed.

Emergency Preparation - The Basics

"In an emergency, generally you tend to think of meeting more basic needs than preferences and flavors," Elizabeth Andress, professor and food safety specialist- University of Georgia.

Whilst it cannot be predicted when a disaster will strike, the better you plan when you begin prepping, the better prepared you will be for dealing with such situations. By practicing prevention, you can mitigate the risk of a disaster.

Being prepared for various types of emergency situations is a part of adapting a provident lifestyle. You can start off by taking into consideration the most likely disasters that could hit your area and plan what you would do in case of these emergencies. It is worthwhile to mention at this stage that emergencies can be classified as short term emergencies and long term emergencies.

Short term emergencies are catastrophic situations that last anywhere from a few hours to a few days. Often we receive a warning about a forthcoming disaster from local authorities. In such situations, we have ample time to get ourselves ready for dealing with a certain situation. Nevertheless, there are situations that cannot be predicted, despite the advancement in the field of science and technology.

If a winter storm, hurricane or an earthquake strikes your community, you might not have access to basic necessities of life such as food, water and electricity for days or even weeks.

Despite the fact that your local government and disaster relief organizations will try to help you in the event of an emergency situation, they may not be able to reach you immediately.

It goes without saying that emergencies can happen anywhere and can have a significant impact on people's lives. Being prepared for an emergency can ensure that you and your family can manage well if confronted with such a situation.

Tropical storms, blizzards, flash floods, whatever the disaster, it pays to be prepared. Disasters like these can disrupt the supply of groceries, food and other critical items. By taking some time to store emergency food supplies and water, you can provide for your entire family.

Decision Making Considerations

There are a number of factors that you should take into consideration when planning for a catastrophic event. While the needs of different family members may vary, your objective should be to have food supplies in your pantry that could last for at least seventy two hours. This should be enough to tide you over until you can get help from the rescue team or relief workers. Additionally, you can begin stockpiling this supply gradually rather than trying to do it all at once.

You need to keep the following questions in consideration as you plan your emergency food supply. It is essential to include all your family members in the decision making process.

What type of foods do you plan to store?

When planning on what types of foods to store, you need to make sure that you list down the inventory of food items that you would require in preparing your favorite family meals. Additionally, it is important for you to consider three basic elements, balance, moderation and variety when planning menus.

The Storage Space: Where do you plan to store the food?

After deciding upon what types of foods to store, the next important question that needs to be answered is, where will you store the food and what storage space do you have for storing food items for emergencies. It is worthwhile to mention at this stage that most food items remain fresh when kept in a cool, dark and dry place. It is important to store food items in containers that are marked as safe and can be used for food storage.

Your Budget: What budget do you have for both supplies and food?

Perhaps the most important question that needs to be answered is what budget you have for food and supplies. This should not be very difficult for you to answer. If you get into a habit of buying a little extra every time you visit your grocery shop, soon you will have an adequate supply of food items in your emergency pantry. On average, a seventy two hours of food supply costs about US$25 per person. This amount, nevertheless; can vary depending upon the kinds of food you select.

Existing Resources: What resources do you already have on hand?

It is also an important to evaluate the resources that you already have on hand including food items as well as alternate sources of cooking in case you are faced with a power outage. From a charcoal barbecue to camp stoves to wood stoves, there are plenty of options available for you to choose from. After carefully evaluating your existing resources and things that you will need to purchase in order to meet the needs of your family, you can plan out your emergency disaster pantry.

Emergency Pantry Basics

The perfect food for the pantry would be some magic pill that contains the complete nutrition and calories of a full meal. But unfortunately, such a magic pill does not exist. Until somebody invents it, you need to make some intelligent choices. You need to group your pantry list into essential items and types of food that you may require during an extended stay at home.

As you stock food, you need to take into consideration, the unique needs of your family. It is important to have familiar foods in your emergency food storage as they boost your morale and give a feeling of security in times of stress. Try to include foods that are enjoyed by your family-foods that are rich in nutrition and calories.

For an emergency survival kit, you should have at least a three day or a seventy two hour supply of non-perishable food items for each member of your household including your pets. Prepackaged foods, canned foods and dry food items such as beans and rice are the easiest to pack and store.

If done before the emergency occurs, preparation for emergency food supplies can be simple. Even though, individuals and family needs may vary, you can use the following basic guidelines to build a food supply for emergency situations.

The Length of Supply
The length of time for which you are preparing your emergency food supply is of prime importance. There are a number of resources available on how to prepare for various food supplies for various lengths of time (the resources can be found in the appendix of this book). Additionally, 'The American Red Cross' is an excellent source of information on disaster preparedness.

Nutritional Considerations
You can include a variety of foods to maintain your nutritional needs and requirements. It is important for you to include foods in your emergency food supply that are familiar to you and your family. When planning your emergency food pantry, it is important to add variety. Be sure that the list covers adequately all the food groups including carbohydrates, proteins and fat.

Perhaps the biggest challenges of surviving on emergency food supplies is that under certain survival situations, you may not have access to fresh food such as fresh vegetables and fruits. As a result, you may find that your diet is lacking some important nutrients such as minerals and vitamins.

A comprehensive list of food is critical in order to determine the nutritional requirements for your family. The minimum requirement should be 2,000 calories per day per person that includes about 20 grams of protein. It is worthwhile to mention at this stage that during stressful situations you need more nutritious food especially protein.

Providing a good variety of meals can prove to be the element that can keep your family strong and emotionally stable during times of stress.

Foods that require little or no effort to prepare or keep
Additionally, foods that do not require special treatments, refrigeration or freezing techniques should be included in your emergency food supplies kit. These may include dried, canned and other non-perishable food.

Building Your Emergency Food Supply

The incident of September 11, 2011, was truly a day of unfortunate tragedy for United States of America- a day of grief, horror and terror for most of us. Incidents like these disrupt our normal life routine leaving us in a state of shock. The feelings of uncertainty, fear and a lost sense of security are some of the most common factors that make catastrophes' very stressful.

So, how can you prepare for whatever your future might hold? The answer is, through building emergency food storage in your home. The best way to prepare is to stock your own grocery store with food supplies that your family likes and rotate these items by using the older ones and replacing the consumed ones with fresh ones.

Should a disaster prevent us from buying food atthe grocery stores, we should be prepared to deal with the situation ourselves. Nevertheless, most households only have a week's supply of food supplies in their pantry. If you had to rely on food supplies in your pantry for an extended period of time you would soon wish that you had a good supply of healthy, nutritious and good tasting ingredients.

Additionally, it is worthwhile to discuss at this stage that fueling your body during a catastrophe is a little different from the diet you consume every day. Since the nutritional requirements and metabolic responses of the body during stressful times are different, you would probably be expending more energy than usual, so you would need high energy and high protein foods in your emergency pantry.

Additionally, because you will have a limited supply of food supplies in your pantry, the higher the quality of foods you eat the better.

Planning for short term emergencies can be as simple as increasing the quantity of non-perishable and staple foods that you normally purchase from your local grocery store. A seventy two hour supply of food should be sufficient for most situations.

However, there might be situations in which you may have to stay confined in your home for extended periods. We will be discussing how you should prepare for short term emergencies as well as long term emergencies in the forthcoming sections of this guide.

Following is a list of some food supplies that you should always have in your emergency pantry. You can begin prepping for emergency situations by stockpiling these foods in your emergency pantry.

FOOD RECOMMENDATIONS

PEANUT BUTTER

In addition to being a good source of protein and fat, peanut butter is a great source of energy. Unless it is mentioned on the label, you do not need to refrigerate it.

WHOLE-WHEAT OR WHOLE GRAIN CRACKERS

Whole wheat crackers offer a good substitute for bread. They can be used to make healthy sandwiches. Nevertheless, because whole grain or whole wheat crackers have a relatively short shelf life in contrast to their counterparts, the fiber enriched crackers work well when you are very hungry.

NUTS AND TRAIL MIXES AND CEREALS

Additionally, you can stock cereals, nuts and trial mixes in your emergency pantry because they are not only healthy but are also convenient for snacking. It is better that you look for vacuum packed mixes which prevents the nuts from oxidizing and keep them fresh for longer periods. It is important that you choose individually packaged multi grain cereals so that they do not become stale once they are opened. These are available in pre-packed packages and you can assemble them on your own.

GRANOLA BARS and POWER BARS

These bars are not only nutritious but they are filling as well. These snacks can stay fresh for a period of at least six months. In addition, these bars also serve as a rich source of carbohydrates.

RAISINS and DRIED FRUITS SUCH AS APRICOT

Raisins and dried fruits are excellent sources of potassium and dietary fiber. You can consume these highly nutritious foods in the absence of fresh foods.

CANNED FOODS TUNA, SALMON, CHICKEN, OR TURKEY

You can also have canned food supplies in your pantry such as canned chicken, tuna, salmon or turkey. These foods have a shelf life of two years and play an important role in providing essential protein that is needed by the human body.

CANNED SOUPS, VEGETABLES AND CHILLI

Additionally, in the absence of fresh food varieties, you can use canned soups, chilli and vegetables to provide you with the essential nutrients. The good part is that you can eat chilli, soups and vegetables straight from the can.

POWDERED FOOD SUPPLIES

Powdered food supplies such as powdered milk serve as excellent food options for your emergency food pantry since they have a relatively long shelf life and can be stored safely for longer periods of time.

SALT, PEPPER AND SUGAR

It goes without saying that your emergency food pantry should have a basic supply of seasonings such as salt, pepper and herbs and sweeteners that are required to flavor the food.

OTHER FOOD OPTIONS

It is wise for you to store comfort foods in your emergency pantry as well including chocolate mixes, cookies, candy bars, canned juices, tea bags, instant coffee etc.

Creating Your Plan and Deciding What You Need

When it comes to buidling an emergency food pantry, a number of people feel overwhelmed at where to begin. With so many varieties available at the food stores, it's easy to get confused.

If you're planning to take the first steps towards building your emergency food storage, it is best to start buying food supplies in small amounts every time you go shopping.

But before purchasing food supplies for your emergency pantry, it is important for you to keep the following rules in consideration. These include;

1. ***Keep a track of what you eat (Breakfast, Lunch and Dinner)*** In order to make the most of your emergency food supply, it is of utmost importance for you to keep a track of what your family eats. This should include your breakfast meals, your lunch meals and dinner meals.

You should take into consideration all the ingredients that are required in the preparation of these meals. You can start off by keeping a track of the food that is consumed by your family in a week. In order to calculate what food supplies you would require if you had to build a three month food supply, multiply it by 13. Similarly, if you want to build a food supply for six months, multiply the ingredients that you would require for the preparation of your family meals by 26.

The advantage of monitoring your daily meals is that this way you will learn what the favorite meals of your family are and shop accordingly. It is essential that you note everything down so that you don't forget anything when you go shopping. In simpler words, it is important that you store foods that your family likes to eat instead of persuading your family to like the foods that you have stored.

2. ***The amount of calories that you take in during emergency situations is critical.*** The second point that you need to take into consideration when building your emergency food storage is the caloric intake in survival situation. As we have discussed it before, emergency situations are stressful events during which your body needs more energy than it normally needs to cope up with the stress.

Therefore, it is of paramount importance for you to stock up on food items that provide your body with the essential nutrients.

3. **Purchase Food Items that can serve more than one purpose.** Additionally, when it comes to purchasing food items for your emergency pantry, it is important for you to buy multifunctional food items than are multifunctional-which means they can be used to prepare a variety of foods. This would also enable you to save a lot of space in your storage pantry. Examples include; Rice, Pasta, beans and wheat.

4. *Stock up on food items that play a vital role in boosting your energy levels.* In addition, it is also important for you to store food items that are rich sources of complex proteins and carbohydrates. These will help boost your energy level and keep your spirits high during a survival situation.

   Examples include; peanut butter, crackers, nuts, trial mixes, granola bars etc. Besides being high energy snacks, these foods have a considerably long shelf life. We will be discussing more about this topic in the next section.

5. *High Protein Food.* Protein is an essential nutrient required by our body during normal situations. It goes without saying that during survival situations, our body requires more protein than it normally does. Therefore, it is important for you to store foods that

are rich in protein including canned meats like tuna, salmon, chicken and ham.

In addition to meat, beans also serve as a good source of protein especially when cooked with rice; they serve as rich source of complex proteins that provide the body with essential amino acids that are required for survival.

6. **Do not forget to stock essential staples.** Staples such as flour, spices, sugar, cooking oil, baking soda and vinegar should always be in your emergency food pantry.

7. **Having pre-packaged meals in your emergency food pantry can offer convenience during stressful situations.** Moreover; having some pre-packaged meals in your emergency pantry will offer convenience during stressful situations. Typically, during an emergency crisis, you need some time before you can get acclimate yourself to cooking in a critical grid down situation.

There are a number of prepackaged food items available at the grocery stores that can offer convenience when you are in a time crunch. Examples include ready-made pancakes, drink mixes and corn breads.

8. **Variety-The Spice of Life.** When building your emergency food storage, it is important for you to

remember that variety is indeed the spice of life. Having a variety of foods stored in your pantry for catastrophic events can prevent the boring monotony that comes with eating the same foods every day. Additionally, having a well-balanced food storage will not only eliminate culinary boredom but will also provide you with a balanced diet.

9. ***Comfort foods.*** In addition to having the essential food supplies in your emergency pantry, it is also important for you to have some comfort foods items-food items that your family enjoys. Examples include; sweet cereals, pudding, pickles, juices, hard candies, apple sauces etc. Comfort foods like these can provide a little bit of normalcy to the catastrophic situation that you may be facing.

10. ***Food Backups.*** In addition, having some back up foods such asfood bars in your emergency food pantry can provide you with greater peace of mind knowing that you have alternative sources of food supply to rely on if you happen to run out of food in your pantry.

MRE's or Meals-Ready-to-eat, offer another food choice to turn to in case you run out of food. Even though, a lot of people do not prefer storing MRE's in their emergency food pantry due to high amount of preservatives, these meals are rich in nutrition and calories.

Note: Bear this in mind that these foods should not be the only food in your emergency food pantry.

The next chapter will help you take a deeper look into the rules of building your emergency food pantry.

Storing Your Food

There are a number of reasons for storing a well-rounded supply of food, water and other essentials. Having adequate food and emergency supplies on hand during a catastrophic situation not only makes you self-sufficient but also brings peace of mind.

This section includes everything that you need to know about stockpiling food for emergency situations. Continue reading to gain an in depth understanding of the basics of food storage.

Food storage simply revolves around the notion of purchasing food supplies and stockpiling them in the home for future use. Following is a list of some points that you need to keep in mind when you begin stockpiling food supplies for emergency situations.

Optimize Your Storage Space-Decide How much Food to Store

Before you could decide on the food supplies that you need to store, it is of paramount importance for you to organize it. It is not only going to give you an idea of how much storage space you have but will also make it easier for you to keep a track of supplies that you have stocked and what you need to store.

Especially if you live in small house or apartment, finding appropriate storage space to stockpile your food can be a challenge. Nevertheless, you can get creative when finding the space in your home for your emergency food supply. You can also consider adding racks, cabinets and shelves for storing various food items. You can visit your local store to get pantry organizers that suit your needs.

Learning how to optimize the storage space in your pantry with organization and space will make the task much easier for you.

Food Storage Tips

Following is a list of storage tips that you need to bear in mind before storing food in your emergency pantry.

- Before stocking up foods, it is important for you to try them out at least once to make sure they match your tastes and culinary preferences. As discussed in the previous section, the best way to prepare is to stock your very own home grocery store with food items that your family likes.
- Secondly, it is important that you continually rotate your food supply and rotate the food items that are consumed with fresh ones so you never run out of food. This is a practical and economical way of storing food in your pantry.
- If you want to store food for a short duration of time, you can consider dehydrating it yourself. Nevertheless, it is important that you consume it every few months and do not store it for longer periods.
- Moreover, you can make your own good old raisins and nuts mix. It not only offers energy but also tastes

good but it can't be kept fresh for longer periods either.

- It is of paramount importance for you to include mineral and vitamin supplements in your pantry in order to ensure that your body gets all the essential nutrients it needs during an emergency situation.
- You can also consider storing powdered milk (which is a good source of calcium), instant noodles (light weight, high caloric and inexpensive).
- Additionally, you can also consider including alternate cooking kits and utensils in your emergency food store.
- While most food supplies stay fresh when stored in a cool dry place, it is important for you to carefully read the food storage instructions on the label.

In the next section, we will be discussing why it is important to have dehydrated and freeze dried food in your emergency food pantry and how you can store them.

Store Dehydrated and Freeze Dried Food

Freeze dried and dehydrated food serve asgood food choices when it comes to emergency food storage. The ready-made freeze dried and dehydrated meals can be prepared in a matter of minutes simply by adding boiling water.

Freeze dried foods are fresh foods that have been flash frozen and then had the water removed. Once they are rehydrated they taste and look like fresh food. They offer a good solution to your long term storage needs. Additionally, these foods have a considerably long shelf life and can be prepared in both hot and cold water in a matter of minutes. From powdered eggs, to instant coffee to soups to freeze dried diced beef, there are a number of freeze dried food supplies available in the market.

Understanding Expiration Dates

Expiration dates can be simply defined as the date before which a food product is considered to be at its best quality and is safe to be consumed. You can find it printed of the packaging of the food item.

The label either says that the product is 'best before' a certain date or 'use within' a certain time period which means that the product can be safely stored within the period mentioned on the label. In order to ensure that food in your pantry is consumed within the expiration dates, it is important that you practice FIFO or first in-first out practice.

This will ensure that the food that you have stored in your pantry is consumed prior to the expiration date. Dry food supplies such as crackers, seasonings and cake mixes etc should always be stored in their original packaging or in air tight containers to ensure that they stay fresh for a longer period of time.

Rotate your Food Supply

It is important to rotate you food supply on a regular basis which means that you use the food items in your pantry, rotate it and restock them. This is perhaps the best way to have the freshest available to you in the event that a disaster strikes.

Additionally, when organizing your emergency food pantry it is important that you arrange food items with the earliest expiration dates at the front so that you can use them first.

In order to ensure that the food items are used within the expiration dates, it is important that you perform an inventory check every six months for all the food items.

Consider Storing MRE's

Meals ready to eat or MRE's are an excellent addition to your emergency food storage. Designed originally for military as survival food, MRE's have a shelf life of five to seven years. These are light weight meals requiring little or no preparation and are easy to store and use. With proper storage these meals can be stored for longer periods of time.

Table 1: Meal Ready-to-eat: Storage Life

Temperatures (F)	Months of Storage
120 ^{0}F	1
110 ^{0}F	5
100 ^{0}F	22
90 ^{0}F	55
80 ^{0}F	76
70 ^{0}F	100
60 ^{0}F	130

Basics of Prepping Your Own Food

Learn Basic Cooking Skills

In order to prepare for dealing with an emergency situation it is important for you to learn basic cooking skills as you might have to use them until the situation is under control.

How to Sprout Beans and Seeds

The process of sprouting involves germination of dormant seeds. These are consumed as young shoots. In addiion to offering all the essential nutrients, sprouting beans and seeds is a very simple and cost effective process.In addition,

1. Growing sprouts indoorsoffers a great way to have healthy, full of nutrition, fresh food irrespective of the outdoor conditions.

2. These are highly nutritious foods as the process of sprouting improve their nutritional profile. In simple words, sprouted foods contain high levels of minerals, proteins, phytochemicals and antioxidants.

3. Sprouting is especially easy to do in case of survival situations and provides a good source of food when food supplies are scarce. Sprouting in survival situation will ensure that you have a nutritious, healthy diet.

4. You can grow a number of sprouts including nuts, grains, beans, vegetables etc.

If you are interested in growing sprouts at your home, there is good news. All you need is seeds of your choice and a suitable glass jar. However, you can also use sprout bags that are made of breathable material or sprouting trays.

The Process

1. Soaking your seeds- In the first step mix 2 to 3 parts of water to 1 part of seed. Make sure that the seeds are well soaked and evenly distributed in water. Let them soak in water for about eight to ten hours. After the process of soaking is done, drain the water and rinse the seeds well.

2. Now place the soaked and rinsed seeds in your sprouting container or tray.

3. Rinse well again .It is important to mention at this stage that rinsing is a process that is done frequently until the process gets completed.

4. After rising it is of paramount importance for you to drain as much water as you can to ensure that your sprouts get the optimum conditions to grow. Every time you rinse your seeds, it is important that you drain them well.

5. Repeat the rinsing and draining process 2-3 times a day until the sprouts reach the desired length. The process normally takes about a week to grow.

How to make Homemade Yogurt

Making yogurt at home is not only simple but is also an economical process and above all if you know how to prepare yogurt at your home it can offer great help during a survival situation.

In order to prepare yogurt at your own home, follow the instructions given below;

1. In the first step boil around half gallon of milk in a cooking pot.

2. Cool it down slightly. (However do not cool it down completely. Make sure that it is still warm).

3. Take 2-3 tablespoons of plain yogurt (to be used as a starter) in a bowl.

4. Gently add in milk.
5. Cover it and place the bowl in warm place.

6. Leave it for 4 – 5 hours and it is ready.

How to Dry Marinate Vegetables

During prolonged periods of emergency, dry marinating may prove to the best choice, primarily because it required less energy and involves very little cost. You can dry marinade both vegetables and meat. All you need to do is to blanch vegetables, and allow them to dry. Then add in the dry spices and herbs (as per recipe) and let it stay for a while so that the marinade soaks well into the food (vegetable or meat).

You can dry these vegetables in a dehydrator or in sunlight (in case you do cannot use a dehydrator). Additionally, you can also consider preserving the marinated vegetables in vinegar and storing them for in jars for extended periods.

Basic Canning Methods

Canning allows preservation of a wide variety of foods, from fruits and vegetables to meats and legumes. It can easily be done at home with either a pressure canner (for most foods) or simply a large pot of boiling water (for fruits and acidic foods).

Basic Canning Rules and Tips

1. You need to carefully wash the jars and their lids before using them. It is of utmost importance for you to sterilize these jars to make sure they do not become contaminated. Sterilize the jars with lids by immersing them in hot water for about ten minutes.

2. Additionally, it is important that you keep the jars and their lids in warm water to avoid explosion when they are put into the hot water present in the canner. Additionally, it is important that you avoid overfilling as it might cause an explosion.

3. After the canning process is done, leave the jars and their lids on a cooling rack. Allow them to cool. It is essential that you leave the jars undisturbed for about twenty four hours after the process to make sure they do not explode.

   You can test the seals of jars using the back of a spoon. Tap the lids to check if they ring. If they ring, the seal is good. If they make a hollow thud, it means the seal is not good.

4. To ensure a long shelf life, it is important to store cans in a cool dry place.

5. Even though, most foods can be canned, it is usually said that the process takes away some of the nutritional content of the food, and the final product usually has a low nutritional profile compared to the original food.

Try Simple Canning Recipes at Home

Canning Tomatoes

1. To can tomatoes, fill in a large saucepan with water. Bring it to a boil. Add in the tomatoes.
2. After you add in the tomatoes, wait for fifteen minutes. As the outer skin of the tomato breaks, take them out and transfer them into cold water. This way becomes easier to peel them.
3. Peel the tomatoes and chop them.
4. Use a canning funnel to put the tomatoes in the jars. (you can find these at Walmart, on Amazon, or anywhere canning supplies are sold)
5. You can add in a pinch of salt if you want.
6. Fill in the jars with water.
7. Cover the jars with lids.
8. Tightly screw on the rims.
9. Add water in the hot water bath canner and bring it to a boil.
10. Put in the jars. Make sure they are covered nicely with water. Process the jars for fifteen minutes and pull them out.
11. Leave the jars undisturbed for about fifteen to twenty minutes to make sure that the lids have sealed properly.

Canning Potatoes

1. Wash and Peel the potatoes.
2. Cut into small cubes.
3. Transfer the diced potatoes in the jars. Make sure they are packed tightly.
4. Add in water leaving about ½ inch headspace.
5. Using a clean muslin cloth, gently clean off the tops of the jars. (This step is essential to forming a proper seal.)
6. Place the lids on jars and tightly screw on the rims.
7. Transfer the jars into a pressure canner.
8. Add in about three quarts of water. Do not put the lid on.
9. Turn on the burner and bring the water to a boil. Once it starts boiling, put on the lid. It is important to make sure that the lid is sealed properly.
10. When putting the lid on do not put the pressure weight on. As you see steam coming out of the canner, put the weight on.
11. The pressure will start to build once you put on the weight.
12. Once the pressure builds, monitor the pressure gauge. When the pressure gauge reads between 10-12 pounds of pressure, set the timer for about forty minutes. Make sure the gauge maintain the pressure range.
13. Cool down the jars for about 1 to 2 hours. (DO NOT try to take the lid off until the unit has cooled down and the pressure has been release – it will explode!)

Canning Cabbages

1. Rinse cabbages and remove and damaged leaves.
2. Cut them into thin strips.
3. Put water in a large bowl and bring it to a boil.
4. Put the sliced cabbage into the jars. Pack the jars firmly as the process of canning will make them softer.
5. Fill the jars with water leaving about ½ inch of headspace.
6. Wipe off the tops of the jars using a muslin cloth. This step is essential to seal them properly.
7. Place the lids on the jars and tightly screw on the rims.
8. Transfer the jars into a pressure canner. Add in about three quarts of water. Do not put the lid on.
9. Turn on the burner and bring the water to a boil. Once it starts boiling, put on the lid. It is important to make sure that the lid is sealed properly.
10. When putting the lid on do not put the pressure weight on. As you see steam coming out of the canner, put the weight on.
11. The pressure will start to build once you put on the weight.
12. Once the pressure builds, monitor the pressure gauge. When the pressure gauge reads between 10-12 pounds of pressure, set the timer for about fifty five minutes. Make sure the gauge maintain the pressure range.
13. Cool down the jars for about 1 to 2 hours.

Canning Oranges

The process of canning oranges is a little different from the canning methods we have discussed until now.

1. In the first step, we will be making light syrup. To prepare the syrup, boil water and add in sugar. Simmer until the sugar gets dissolved. Keep the syrup warm until the oranges are ready to be packed in this syrup.
2. Next, peel the oranges using a citrus peeler and separate the slices (be sure to remove all of the white membrane called the pith – otherwise the oranges will turn bitter).
3. Pack the jars with orange slices leaving about ½ inch of headspace.
4. Add in the syrup, again leaving about ½ inch of headspace.
5. Before adding the lids, gently clean off the rims of the jars. This is an important step that will ensure that the jars are sealed properly.
6. Add the lids and the rims. Make sure that the rims are screwed tight.
7. Before adding in the jars, preheat the water. You do not need to bring it to a boil. Add in the jars. Make sure the jars are covered properly with water.
8. Simmer the jars for a good ten to fifteen minutes. Turn off the heat and allow the water to cool down before the jars can be taken out.
9. Once you take them out, leave them on the counter undisturbed.
10. Leave them undisturbed for several hours until they are sealed well.

Canning Chicken

1. Before you can begin the canning procedure, it is important that you clean the chicken well. If you've butchered your own chicken, make sure it does not have feathers or blood on it.
2. In the next step, cut the chicken into pieces and put it in a Crockpot.
3. Add in water and let the chicken cook for about 8- 10 hours.
4. After the chicken is cooked, transfer it to a bowl and shred it into small pieces. Remove the bones.
5. Add the de-boned chicken into jars. Make sure the jars are only half filled with chicken, so that there is room for the broth you have prepared.
6. Add in the broth leaving about ½ inch of headspace in the jar.
7. Gently clean the rims of the jars and add in the rims and lids on the jars.
8. It is important to make sure that the rims are screwed tightly.
9. Place the jars in the pressure canner. It is important for you to understand that meat needs to be pressure canned as a simple hot water bath is not enough to make the meat safe to store at room temperature.

Note: Follow the directions given on your individual canner.

Drying Herbs and Peppers without Using a Dehydrator

Drying herbs is no doubt the easiest method to preserve them. From rosemary to cilantro to basil to dill, almost any herb can be dried using simple techniques. A dehydrator is not necessarily required.

If you have your own herb garden at your home, you can easily pick these herbs and use them for cooking. Additionally, you can also make these herbs available during the winter season when your herb garden is not that green. Drying herbs is perhaps the easiest way to have a good quality supply of herbs throughout the year. Drying these herbs at home will also make sure that the final product is of highest quality in contrast to the herbs available in the market.

In order to retain their quality and flavor, you can use the air drying technique which offers the most inexpensive and easiest methods of preserving herbs. Even though through this technique the moisture present in the herbs evaporates very slowly. The air drying procedure retains the essential oils present in the herbs even after the drying process.

Dehydrators can be used when you are drying large quantities of herbs or herbs with high moisture content such as basil. Herbs with low moisture content such as thyme, sage, dill, oregano, marjoram, rosemary and summer savory are some of the herb varieties that can be dried using air drying techniques.

If you try to air dry herbs with higher moisture content it is more likely they will mold if they are not air dried properly and quickly. In addition, putting herbs in a paper bag and making holes in the bags for air circulation will protect the herbs from pollutants and dust.

The perfect time to cut the herbs for the drying process is just before they flower. This is the stage when the leaves have the most oil which gives them the flavor and aroma. The flowering season of different herbs is different, so it would be very difficult for you to identify if they are in their flowering season. To get an idea, look for the newly opened flowers or buds. Nevertheless, there is no hard and fast rule. You can also air dry herbs when they have already flowered.

In order to air dry herbs, follow this simple procedure outlined below;

1. Using a sharp knife cut large branches or stems from mature plants. To remove insects, shake each branch gently. Carefully remove diseased, damaged old leaves.
2. Rinse the branches that you have cut in cold water and pat them dry using a paper towel. It is important for you to remember that wet herbs have a tendency to destroy the entire branch or stem.
3. In the next step, turn these branches or stems upside down and remove leaves present along the upper stem.
4. Next, take five to six stems together and tie them. It will appear as a small bunch. If you are drying high moisture herbs, keep the bunch even smaller.
5. Now place the bunch upside down in a big paper bag. Make small holes in the bag for ventilation.
   Additionally, it is also important for you to make sure that there is enough space in the bag for the air to circulate. Make sure that the leaves do not touch the bag.

6. Now hang the bag in a nice warm and airy room. Leave them untouched for about two weeks (longer if needed).
7. Monitor them regularly in order to keep a check on mold growth.
8. When the drying process is completed, check the leaves again for mold growth.
9. Once you are sure that there is no mold growth, strip the leaves from the stem. Discard the stems.
10. You can crush the leaves if you want, but bear this important point in mind that whole leaves retain their flavors for a longer period of time than when they are ground, crushed or rubbed.
11. Store the dried herbs in air tight containers. Store them away from light and moisture. You can also use zip closure bags, or other containers for storing dried herbs.
12. Dried herbs can be stored for longer periods but most the flavor and aroma of herbs diminishes with time and you more quantity will be required to achieve the desired flavor and aroma. The only exception is sage, which intensifies in flavor during storage.
13. To get the full flavor, crush the dried leaves just before adding them to your recipe.

Conclusion

It goes without saying that disasters strike with little or no warning and can leave tremendous amount of destruction and ruin in their wake. Survivors, nevertheless; can get through even the toughest circumstances using the right information and tools. Knowing which type of disasters could affect your area will help your plan more thoroughly for the disaster.

Whilst the advancement in the field of science and technology may lead us to a reasonable understanding of some phenomenon, it does not unfortunately translate into an accurate prediction capability.

You need to remember, the primary purpose of building an emergency food pantry is to;

- Develop skills to survive worse circumstances
- Prepare for the unthinkable, and
- Keep your family safe and secure

By actively preparing for an emergency crisis in which the basic necessities of life are scarce, you would know exactly what action needs to be taken during a particular situation. How comforting is that?

Having an understanding of this information and being able to utilize it during catastrophic situations could actually mean the difference between life and death. From common mistakes to avoid to comprehensive list of foods that you should store for emergencies, the book will help you learn the preparedness lifestyle by approaching emergency planning and preparedness in a systematic step by step manner.

Stay Safe!

Macenzie

Please leave a review and let us know what you liked about this book by going to https://www.amazon.com/gp/css/order-history *then clicking on Orders.*

Check out the other *"Survival Family Basics"* Titles...

The Beginner Prepper's Guide for When Disaster Strikes

http://www.amazon.com/dp/B00HG7Y4YS

The Prepper's Emergency First Aid & Survival Medicine Handbook

http://www.amazon.com/dp/B00I90UPSK

The Hunkering Down Guide to Protect and Defend Your Home When Disaster Strikes

http://www.amazon.com/dp/B00J1VGJXG

The Prepper Survival Guide to Bugging Out When it's Time to Get Out of Dodge

http://www.amazon.com/dp/B00J1V939S

References

- U.S. Fire Administration – www.usfa.dhs.gov
- Citizen Corps – www.citizencorps.gov
- U.S. Centers for Disease Control & Prevention – www.cdc.gov
- U.S. Department of Energy – www.energy.gov
- U.S. Department of Homeland Security – www.ready.gov
- U.S. Environmental Protection Agency – www.epa.gov
- National Weather Service – www.nws.noaa.gov
- U.S. Nuclear Regulatory Commission – www.nrc.gov
- American Red Cross – www.redcross.org
- Federal Emergency Management Agency – www.fema.gov
- http://www.getprepared.gc.ca/cnt/rsrcs/pblctns/yprprdnssgd/index-eng.aspx
- http://www.thenewsurvivalist.com/golden_rule_of_food_storage.html